SEARCH THE PAGE

FOR KIDS 3-5

FUN TO FIND!

KRISSY BONNING-GOULD

ILLUSTRATED BY GARETH WILLIAMS

R

ROCKRIDGE
PRESS

THIS BOOK BELONGS TO:

For general information on our other products and services or to obtain technical support, please contact our Customer Care Department within the United States at (866) 744-2665, or outside the United States at (510) 253-0500.

Rockridge Press publishes its books in a variety of electronic and print formats. Some content that appears in print may not be available in electronic books, and vice versa.

Interior and Cover Designer: Brieanna Hattey Felschow
Art Producer: Hannah Dickerson
Editor: Cathy Hennessy
Production Editor: Mia Moran
Illustrations © 2020 Gareth Williams
Illustrator photo courtesy of Advocate Art

ISBN: Print 978-1-64876-259-8

R0

There is so much to see in our big world when you take the time to look around. Let's go on a search-and-find adventure! Together we'll find fireflies at a nighttime campsite, search for animals on the family farm, spot a dump truck at a busy construction site, and even see a few seahorses at the aquarium.

So, are you ready for some search-and-find fun? You never know what you'll find!

So Many Musical Instruments!

It's time for music class, and there are so many instruments to play.

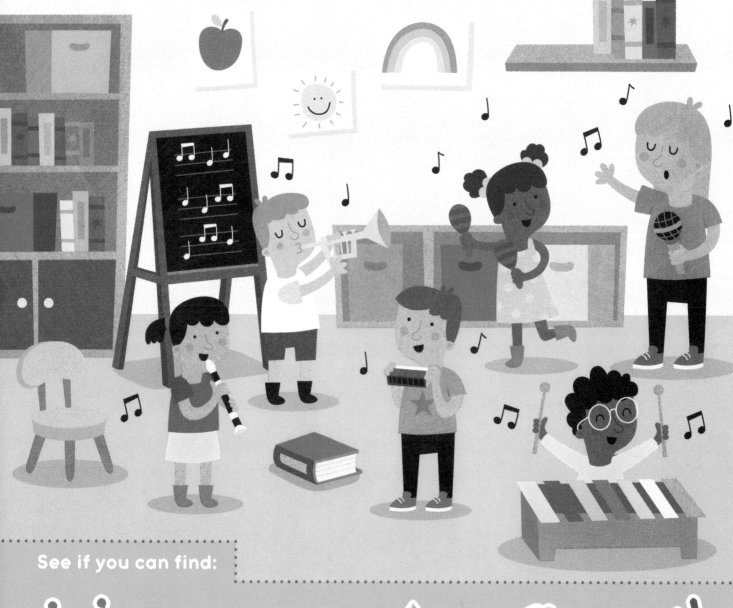

See if you can find:

yellow drum

harmonica

trumpet

tambourine

handbells

2 maracas

green guitar

recorder

2 shaker eggs

xylophone

Camping Under the Stars

The camping fun continues after the stars come out!

See if you can find:

moon

firewood

3 fireflies

shooting star

lantern

banjo   blue book   flashlight   puppy   owl

Snow Day, Family Day

It's a winter wonderland outdoors! Let's go out to play in the snow.

See if you can find:

snowballs

red bird

hot chocolate

green boots

orange sled

mittens   striped scarf   snow shovel   earmuffs   3 buttons

A Grand Garden

Spring has arrived! Grandpa and Grandma need help planting a garden.

See if you can find:

gardening gloves

robin

bumblebee

seed packet

watering can

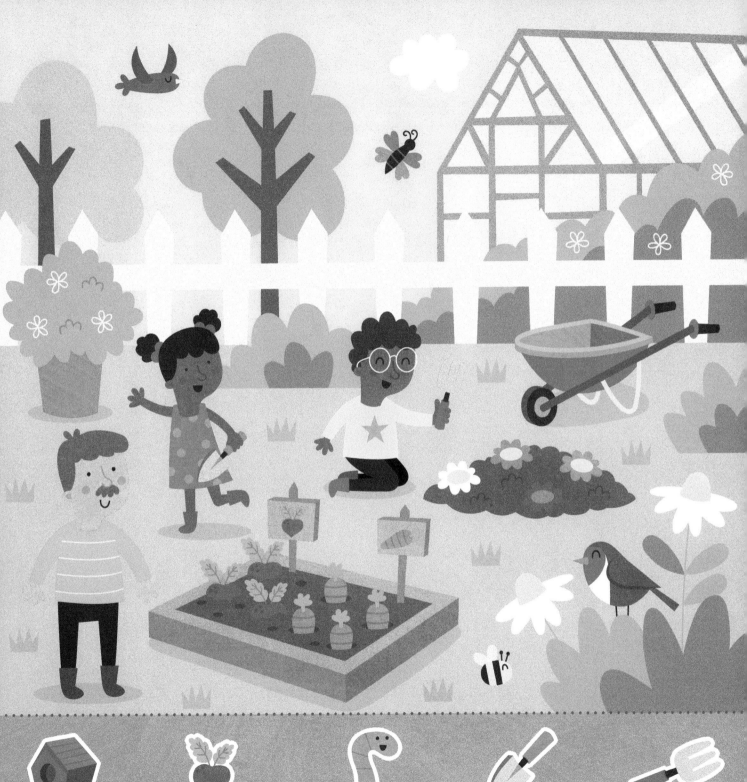

birdhouse

4 beets

worm

shovel

rake

Beach Blast!

Let's have some summer fun in the sun at the beach.
We'll swim and build sandcastles!

See if you can find:

 big beach ball

 sunscreen

 3 seashells

 water bottle

 red crab

sunglasses

flip-flops

sandcastle

life jacket

beach umbrella

Fall Family Fun!

Fall is for hayrides, pumpkins, and apple picking.
Let's join the family fun at the orchard.

See if you can find:

chipmunk

6 pumpkins

tractor

letter A

green apple

APPLES

FRESH CIDER

basket

blue jay

small sunflower

jug of cider

scarecrow

Batter Up!

It's fun to play baseball with friends—no matter who wins. You're up next to bat!

See if you can find:

baseball

number 2

red cap

butterfly

striped pants

hot dog **star** **square sign** **blue glove** **bat**

Storytime at the Library

Let's meet at the library for storytime and then borrow some books to take home.

BOOKS ARE ROARSOME!

See if you can find:

toy train   2 purple books   library card   letter T   rainbow

recycling bin

book cart

laptop

dinosaur

eyeglasses

Dog Park

The dog park sure is busy today!
There are so many different kinds of dogs.

See if you can find:

 big bone

 newspaper

 square sign

 5 tulips

yellow ball

 nest

 purple collar

 water dish

 squirrel

 Frisbee

On Stage

Let's join the puppet theater fun!
Shh...the show is about to start.

PUPPET SHOW

See if you can find:

2 buttons

an arrow

GLUE

glue

polka-dot tie

6

number 6

markers **triangle flag** **3 stars** **green bow** **pink sock**

NEXT SHOW AT 6PM

Learning Is Fun!

There are so many fun things to learn at school! Let's see what these students are doing.

See if you can find:

red apple

number 3

backpack

box of crayons

clock

globe

yellow ruler

painting easel

letter X

microscope

Little Gym

Jump, climb, tumble, and stretch.
Let's get moving at the gym!

BE SAFE

See if you can find:

trampoline

Hula-Hoop

striped shirt

arrow

green mat

| diamond | purple shoes | balance beam | bow | 2 rings |

Lake Life

The lake is busy with wildlife today!
Let's go on a boat ride to get a better view.

See if you can find:

letter R

3 seagulls

orange fish

frog

rabbit

LAKE WALTERS

 sun hat

turtle

1 oar

cattails

  4 ducklings

The Family Farm

There's always so much happening at the family farm!
Let's help take care of the animals.

See if you can find:

straw hat

10 eggs

4 sheep

black heart

wheelbarrow

rooster

5 hay bales

gray cat

weather vane

blue overalls

Let's Celebrate!

Spending time with friends is the best gift of all.
Let's join the party!

See if you can find:

grapes

number 4

pink cupcake

4 candles

piñata

crown

green balloon

teddy bear

letter B

small present

Choo, Choo!

All aboard for some wooden railroad play!
This train is about to leave the station.

See if you can find:

red train   **conductor hat**   **stop sign**   **9 trees**   **logs**

a sun

railroad crossing

number 5

bridge

crane

Grocery Helper

Time to go grocery shopping!
Can you help find everything on the list?

See if you can find:

| cheese | pineapple | 3 cartons of milk | peanut butter | cabbage |

FRESH FOOD

BREAD

EGGPLANT

PINEAPPLE

5 cans of soup

4 loaves of bread

watermelon

6 eggplants

8 lemons

Playground Pals

It's a sunny day. Let's join some friends at the playground!

See if you can find:

tire swing

mushroom

ladder

5 daffodils

sand bucket

big slide

airplane

2 triangle flags

visor

little slide

Hard at Work!

The construction crew is building a new town post office. It's fun to see the machines at work!

POST OFFICE

See if you can find:

excavator

white hard hat

crane

triangle sign

dump truck

3 shovels

tape measure

loader

9 safety cones

concrete mixer

So Many Sea Animals

Let's go on a field trip to the aquarium and see how many sea animals we can spot!

See if you can find:

starfish

big shark

5 fish

octopus

eel

3 seahorses

stingray

small sea turtle

jellyfish

orange coral

Just Imagine!

Playing dress-up is so much fun!
What would you like to pretend to be?

See if you can find:

letter S

necklace

polka-dot apron

cowboy hat

tutu

IMAGINE

magic wand   orange handbag   wings   police badge   fox costume

3, 2, 1, Blast Off!

Let's spend the day exploring the Air and Space Museum. There is so much to see and do!

See if you can find:

aviator hat

camera

Earth

number 2

airplane propeller

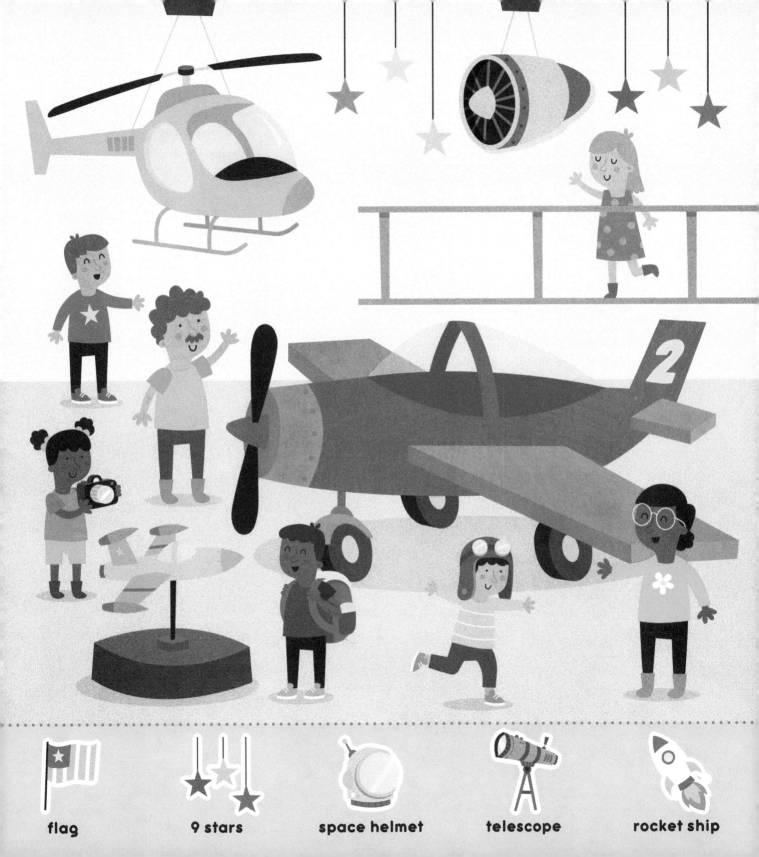

flag   **9 stars**   **space helmet**   **telescope**   **rocket ship**

Carnival Fun!

Carnivals are full of fun games, exciting rides, and yummy food. What do you want to try first?

TICKETS

See if you can find:

pink teacup

popcorn

zebra

1 2 3
4 5 6

numbers 1 to 6

H

letter H

cotton candy

8 milk bottles   **green cap**   **lightning bolt**

5 balloons

About the Author

Krissy Bonning-Gould is a former art teacher with a master's degree in K-12 art education. After becoming a mother, Krissy founded the popular site *B-Inspired Mama* where she shares inspiration for kids' crafts, learning fun, kid-friendly recipes, and creative parenting tips. Krissy is also the author of *The Outdoor Toddler Activity Book, The Rainy Day Toddler Activity Book, Toddler Activities Made Easy*, and *My First Animal Activity Book*. Follow her educational fun at B-InspiredMama.com and on Twitter, Instagram, and Pinterest at @BInspiredMama.

About the Illustrator

Gareth Williams lives in London with his amazing wife. From an early age he loved to draw, and that passion continues to this day. It's something he still can't believe he gets to do for a living! Gareth's illustrated everything from greeting cards to editorial illustrations and children's books. He loved working on this book and hopes the objects aren't too easy to find. You can follow his work on Instagram at @gareth.designs.

Printed in the USA
CPSIA information can be obtained
at www.ICGtesting.com
LVHW061322171223
766457LV00003B/35

9 781648 762598